OLDBUR\
AND
ROWLEY REGIS
IN OLD PHOTOGRAPHS

BIRMINGHAM STREET, Oldbury, from the elevated section of the M5 motorway. The tower of the parish church is prominent in this view.

OLDBURY
AND
ROWLEY REGIS
IN OLD PHOTOGRAPHS

COLLECTED BY
JOHN MADDISON

ALAN SUTTON

Alan Sutton Publishing Limited
Phoenix Mill · Far Thrupp · Stroud · Gloucestershire

First Published 1991

British Library Cataloguing in Publication Data

Oldbury and Rowley Regis in old photographs.
1. Maddison, John
942.49

ISBN 0-86299-976-6

Typeset in 9/10 Korinna.
Typesetting and origination by
Alan Sutton Publishing Limited.
Printed in Great Britain by
The Bath Press, Avon.

CONTENTS

THE ROWLEY HILLS are formed of basalt, a hard volcanic rock, known locally as 'Rowley Rag', which is particularly suitable for road making. It is thought that the first stone was quarried in the district over 2,000 years ago, its earliest use being in the construction of boundary walls. Quarrying on a commercial basis began around 1820 and is carried out today on a large scale. This view shows Rowley Hall Quarry around the turn of the century, with the hall itself visible on the horizon.

INTRODUCTION

This book covers the area on the southern edge of the Black Country represented by the former municipal boroughs of Oldbury and Rowley Regis. Belonging historically to different counties, the two were brought together under one authority by local government reforms of the 1960s and 1970s. Both are made up of several smaller districts, each with its own distinct character, and it is upon these districts that the various chapters are based.

Oldbury originally formed part of Halesowen Manor, which was Crown property held by Roger, Earl of Shrewsbury at the time of the Domesday survey. Roger subsequently annexed the manor to Shropshire and most of the district formed a detached portion of that county until 1844 when it was finally transferred to Worcestershire. In 1214 King John granted the manor to the Bishop of Winchester for the foundation of a religious house and thereafter it came under the control of Halesowen Abbey. The Manor of Oldbury did not have a separate existence until after the dissolution, when it was held by Sir Robert Dudley. Blakeley Hall, close to the boundary with Smethwick, was the manor house.

Ecclesiastically, Oldbury formed part of Halesowen parish until 1841. Christ Church, completed in that year, was built partly with proceeds from the sale of enclosed lands. The original chapel of ease stood on the site of the public buildings and was built and maintained at the expense of the people of Oldbury.

Oldbury owes its industrial pre-eminence to its mineral resources, now exhausted, and to its position on James Brindley's Birmingham Canal, completed in 1772. The earliest enterprise of note was the Brades Works, which began life in the 1860s as a group of blacksmiths' forges. With the coming of the canal, firms which had earlier established themselves in Birmingham sought sites in Oldbury on which to build new factories and expand production. The manufacturing output of the town is diverse, but particular mention should be made of the chemical industry, which began in the early nineteenth century, and the steel tube industry, introduced at the beginning of the present century.

Langley was known as the Manor of Walloxhall in the sixteenth century, but it is unlikely that it ever had an independent existence and it has certainly formed part of Oldbury since that time. It had been largely built up by the beginning of the twentieth century. The area is part industrial and part residential.

Warley, which forms the southern part of Oldbury, was largely rural until the mid-1920s. In 1928 a large portion, including Warley Woods Park, was transferred from Oldbury to Smethwick County Borough for housing purposes, and by the outbreak of the Second World War the district had become almost entirely residential. For the sake of completeness, this volume covers the whole area, including parts which have come to be regarded as belonging to Smethwick.

Rowley was included under the lands of the Bishop of Chester in the Domesday survey, but by the end of the twelfth century it was part of the Crown demesne. In 1300 the manor was held by John de Somery. On his death, in 1321, it was divided between his sisters, Margaret and Joan, one part becoming Rowley Somery and the other Rowley *Regis*. Rowley Regis was granted to Halesowen Abbey during the reign of Edward III. The manor house itself was at Brickhouse, to the north of the village.

Until the nineteenth century, Rowley church was a chapel of ease attached to the parish of Clent. The distance between the two gave rise to much inconvenience, particularly with the growth in population of Rowley. They were eventually separated by a Private Act of 1841, largely through the efforts of the redoubtable George Barrs, curate of Rowley Regis, who was also responsible for replacing the thirteenth-century church.

Rowley village lies clustered around the church on the southern approach to the hills. During the nineteenth century most of the villagers were engaged in the traditional Black Country trade of nailmaking, most houses having a small forge in place of a wash-house and much of the work being carried out by women. The village retained its somewhat quaint appearance until the 1950s, but since then road improvements and housing development have robbed it of much of its character.

To the south lies the shopping centre of Blackheath, until the mid-nineteenth century a sparsely inhabited district of heathland with a few small farms. It developed rapidly following the sale of the parish glebe land in 1841 and soon outstripped the old village as the local centre of population.

Old Hill and Cradley Heath together from the south-western part of Rowley Regis. Despite its name Old Hill is a low-lying district. The coal measures reach an exceptional thickness at this point and land on either side of the Dudley Canal, in the vicinity of Waterfall Lane, was extensively scarred by mining activity. By contrast, the district immediately to the south, around Haden Hill, remained relatively unspoilt and developed into an attractive residential district. Cradley Heath was the centre of the Black Country chainmaking industry and the home of the New British Iron Company, the largest undertaking in the region during the nineteenth century.

To the north of the Rowley Hills, on the borders of Tipton and West Bromwich, lies Tividale, once a mining district, but now occupied by housing estates and modern factories. This district is somewhat isolated from the rest of Rowley and is more closely linked with the neighbouring towns. Included in Tividale for the purposes of this book are some of the scattered settlements which lie in the northern part of the Rowley Hills.

Both towns became urban districts in 1894 and municipal boroughs in the 1930s. In 1966 they were combined with Smethwick to form the County Borough of Warley, which was itself merged with West Bromwich to form the Metropolitan Borough of Sandwell in 1974. Oldbury is poised to become the administrative hub of the borough with a new civic centre soon to open in the town centre.

The photographs in this book have been drawn from a variety of sources, and cover a span of around a hundred years, the most recent dating from the early 1970s. They provide a fascinating glimpse into the life and work of generations of Black Country folk and will be of interest to both the student of local history and the casual reader.

Oldbury

'THE BIG HOUSE', in Church Street, is probably the oldest building in Oldbury. It bears the date 1705 above the doorway, although parts of the house are almost certainly earlier. It has been used as offices since 1857, but was formerly occupied by the Palmer family, descendants of William Freeth.

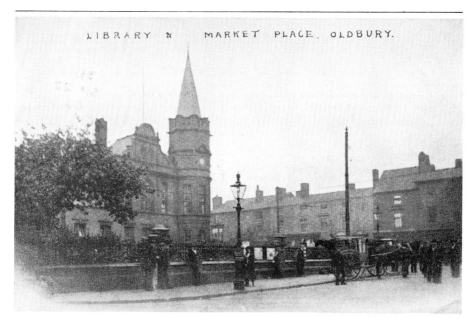

MARKET SQUARE, showing the public buildings erected in 1890/1 to the designs of Wood & Kenrick, of West Bromwich. The gardens which formed part of the original churchyard can be seen in the upper view. These had been removed by the time the lower photograph was taken in 1935.

Save a centre now occupy about site

TWO PHOTOGRAPHS OF THE MARKET SQUARE taken from a window of the public buildings in the early 1930s. The Talbot Hotel and the war memorial erected in 1929 appear in the lower view.

THE OLD TALBOT (left), in Birmingham Street, was built in 1759 and is thought to have been a coaching house on the road from Birmingham to Dudley. Following closure in 1961, the building stood derelict for over twenty years prior to demolition. Built in 1845, the Talbot Hotel (below), overlooking the Market Square, was the largest and most important hostelry in the town. In its early years it acted as the venue for meetings of the Court Leet of the Manor of Oldbury. Despite having listed building status, it was closed in 1969 and pulled down during the following year. Both photographs were taken in 1968.

Margaret & Gary's wedding reception was held here.

FOSTER BROTHERS LTD, gents' outfitters, at the corner of Church Street and Freeth Street, in the early 1890s. In later years the firm had a shop in Halesowen Street. Note the unusual pillar box.

F. BLACKHAM'S DRUG STORES, 53 Birmingham Street. It was common before the First World War for chemists to offer a dental service. This usually involved little more than the extraction of teeth; an operation which Mr Blackham undertook to perform 'carefully'.

W.K. ADAMS & SONS LTD, the largest store in Oldbury, was established in 1891 when William Keys Adams took over 'The Old Established Drapery Warehouse' of Mr T.E. Cooper in Birmingham Street. Capital for the venture was provided by Thomas Frost, the Birmingham draper to whom Adams had been apprenticed from 1880, and the firm originally traded as Frost & Adams. In later years, the business outgrew the small shop (left) and expanded to take over adjoining premises in Birmingham Street and Low Town. The store was rebuilt in 1926 and altered little in appearance until declining trade brought about its closure in 1969 (below).

BIRMINGHAM STREET under snow prior to the First World War.

POLLY ON THE FOUNTAIN was the popular name given to the cast iron statue surmounting the drinking fountain which stood in Birmingham Street, close to the Junction Inn. It was given to the town by 'Squire' David Taylor, founder of the London Ironworks, in 1882. Both the fountain and the statue were cast at the Coalbrookdale Iron Company's Works at Ironbridge, the figure being named 'Europe' in the manufacturer's catalogue. Polly was a feature of the town centre for over sixty years until she was knocked from her plinth by drunken revellers emerging from the nearby Junction Inn on Christmas Eve 1949. The fountain and troughs were dismantled shortly after and Polly was subsequently handed over to a descendant of David Taylor. She now reposes in a garden in Wiltshire, minus her right arm. Visible in the background is the first branch of Lloyds Bank to be opened outside Birmingham. Lloyds were persuaded to open the branch in 1864 by Albright & Wilson following a number of robberies from vehicles carrying wages for their workforce from the city.

CHRIST CHURCH was built in 1840/1 to replace the old chapel which stood in the Market Square on the site of the public buildings. The chapel-of-ease belonging to Halesowen parish had been erected in 1529 at the expense of the inhabitants of Oldbury. Christ Church is constructed of brick with stone dressings and has seating for over 1,000 people. The surrounding square is now a conservation area.

INTERIOR OF THE ROMAN CATHOLIC CHURCH OF ST FRANCIS XAVIER in Pinfold Street. The church was erected in 1865 and served for exactly one hundred years until its replacement by a new building in McKean Road.

THE WESLEY CHAPEL, in Church Street, dates from 1853. It replaced an earlier chapel in New Meeting Street which had stood since 1800. Today the 1853 building is occupied by the New Testament Church of God.

THE METHODIST TABERNACLE, from which Tabernacle Street took its name, was built in 1870 and replaced an earlier building on the site. It was founded by a group of Methodists who had seceded from Oldbury Wesleyan Church in 1834 and subsequently formed themselves into a society of the Methodist New Connexion. The chapel was demolished when the town centre was redeveloped in the late 1970s. It was photographed in 1968.

THE COURT HOUSE AND POLICE STATION, shown here in 1968, dates largely from the 1860s. A court was first established in Oldbury under an Act of 1807. The ground floor has been used as a library since 1979, but the upper floor was in use as a magistrates' court until recently.

OLDBURY FIRE STATION, Perrott Street, at the time of its opening by Worcestershire County Fire Brigade in June 1952. It was replaced by a new fire station at Birchley motorway junction in 1974.

OLDBURY'S FIRST CINEMA was The Palace (above), shown in 1968 following conversion to a bingo hall. It was opened in November 1910 by James Tyrer, licensee of The White Swan in Church Street, a public house noted for its music hall entertainment. Following several changes of ownership it was acquired by Charles Dent in 1919, who replaced the original building with a much larger hall. It closed as a cinema in 1961. The Savoy (right), seen in 1967, had its origins in the Picturedrome which opened in the old Market Hall, in Birmingham Street, in 1911. Later known as the Picture House, it was entirely rebuilt in the 1920s. Closure came in 1958 and the building was demolished in 1970.

THE PREMISES OF F. HOLDCROFT, FARRIER, in Birmingham Road, on the corner of Broadwell Road.

BIRMINGHAM ROAD in the 1920s, looking towards Anchor Bridge. The M5 motorway now crosses the road at this point.

STONE STREET, from the junction with Green Street, before and after alterations made in the 1920s.

HOUSES IN GREEN STREET condemned under the Slum Clearance Order of 1936, seen from Birmingham Road. Council houses were subsequently built on the site.

BELL FOLD, at Rood End, in the 1930s.

BLAKELEY HALL FARM stood close to the site of Oldbury Manor House. The hall was originally a grange belonging to Halesowen Abbey with a small chapel attached. Oldbury probably did not become a separate manor until 1557, after the dissolution of the Abbey, when Sir Robert Dudley and his wife, the ill-fated Amy Robsart, took possession. On the break-up of the Dudley barony in the seventeenth century, Oldbury passed into the hands of the Cornwallis family. The original hall was a fourteenth century half-timbered building with a moat. It was situated further from the road than the later farmhouse and appears to have survived until around 1768. The photograph was taken in 1934, shortly before the farm buildings were demolished.

BURY HILL PARK was opened in 1897 on land given to the town by John W. Wilson MP. The Lodge and Keeper's House were the gift of Mrs Wilson. Although situated in Oldbury, Bury Hill geologically forms part of the Rowley Hills.

ROUNDS GREEN SCHOOLS in Brades Road, were erected in 1910 and are still in use.

THE BIRMINGHAM CANAL, opened throughout in 1722, passed around the centre of Oldbury in the form of a loop. With the opening of the loop bypass in 1858 it became impossible to enter the town without crossing a canal. This 1927 photograph of canalside cottages was taken from beneath Church Street bridge.

STONE STREET CANAL BRIDGE in the 1920s, prior to rebuilding.

THE BOATYARD OF THOMAS CLAYTON (OLDBURY) LTD, near Tat Bank Road, opened in 1889.
These photographs, taken in 1958, show (above) a tar boat from Walsall Gasworks
negotiating a sharp turn to the foot of Oldbury locks and (below) the narrow boat *Spey*. The
yard closed in 1966.

RECONSTRUCTION OF THE RAILWAY BRIDGE at Oldbury and Bromford Lane station (above) in the mid-1930s. The Birmingham, Wolverhampton & Stour Valley Railway opened in 1852 and was absorbed by the London & North Western Railway fifteen years later. In the lower view, an electric multiple unit is seen arriving at the station, then named Oldbury, on a Stafford-Birmingham service in February 1975. The station was enlarged in 1984 and renamed Sandwell and Dudley.

CHEMICAL WORKS of Chance & Hunt Ltd and Albright & Wilson Ltd seen from the 'Blue Billy' mound in the early 1960s. Chance & Hunt was established in 1835 as an offshoot of Chance's glass works at Smethwick; it became part of ICI in 1926. Albright & Wilson's works opened in 1851 when Arthur Albright moved his phosphorous producing business from Birmingham.

THE LAST STEAM RAILWAY LOCOMOTIVE to work in the Black Country was this Peckett 0–4–0 saddle tank, built in 1902, which was owned by Albright & Wilson. It was last used for shunting at the chemical works in 1973 and subsequently presented to the Chasewater Light Railway.

'BLUE BILLY', the enormous mound of industrial waste which lay between Churchbridge and Park Lane, was the result of tipping by nearby chemical works. These photographs show it in 1966, when it was finally removed and used to fill in the marlhole on which the electricity sub-station now stands. The temporary bridge across Churchbridge connecting the two sites can be seen in the lower view.

Richardson Bro did this work

SLEEPING CARRIAGE constructed at the Broadwell Works of the Oldbury Railway Carriage & Wagon Co. Ltd for the railways of Argentina around the turn of the century. The carriage works opened in 1854 and was the largest employer in the town prior to its closure in 1930.

BRITISH INDUSTRIAL PLASTICS LTD, of Popes Lane, was founded in 1904 as the British Cyanides Co. Ltd. From the mid-1920s the firm experimented with the production of synthetic resins and by the middle of the following decade it had become one of the leading producers of plastics. This photograph showing a tanker leaving the works was taken in 1971.

Leyland Beaver Truck

LONDON WORKS (BARLOWS) LTD, originally known as the Ebenezer Works, began life as an iron works but was later converted to steel rolling. The works was purchased from the receiver by Mr C.T. Barlow in 1932. The general view (above) was taken from the tower of the parish church in 1948, and the lower photograph shows the rolling mill in operation in 1936.

MOSAIC OF STEEL TUBE SECTIONS made at the works of Accles & Pollock Ltd. The company's origins lie in a short-lived venture begun by George Accles, an American engineer, at Holford Mill, Perry Barr, towards the end of the last century. This first attempt to exploit the new process of cold steel drawing was not a financial success, but in 1899 the business was revived by Charles Barlow, formerly secretary to Accles, under the name of Accles Tube Syndicate. It became known as Accles & Pollock in 1901 when financial support was provided by Tom Pollock. The following year the company moved to Churchbridge, Oldbury, and began to expand. Land was purchased in 1909 which was to form the basis of the Paddock works and the firm became part of Tube Investments Ltd in 1919. Additional factory space was acquired in the 1930s when Tube Investments acquired the Broadwell Works for use by its subsidiaries, following the closure of Oldbury Carriage Works.

Langley

BLINDFOLD FARM, or 'Dumb Sal's' Farm, in Causeway Green Road, stood between Hadley Street and the Hen and Chickens public house, roughly on the site of the present Grosvenor Road. It was farmed by Jack Hadley, whose family owned a number of shops and businesses in the Causeway Green area. The farm seems to have disappeared during the 1890s.

HOLY TRINITY CHURCH (above) was consecrated in 1852 and served as the parish church for Langley until 1890, when the much larger church of St Michael and All Angels (below) was built in Causeway Green Road. Holy Trinity closed in 1960 and was subsequently demolished.

Edna and Betty married here

WHYLEY STREET, with Spring Street on the right, in 1970, prior to the redevelopment of the Langley district.

DERELICT BETHEL CHAPEL, in Whyley Street, in 1970. Built in the 1850s, it was converted into a schoolroom following the construction of a new chapel at the corner of Broad Street and Arden Grove in 1877.

HIGH STREET (above), looking towards Station Road, and Station Road (below) from the junction with High Street. Few of the buildings shown in these 1970 photographs remain standing.

THE LANGLEY CLUB AND INSTITUTE HALL, in High Street, was built in 1875 as a Temperance Hall. The Langley Literary and Debating Society, forerunner of the Institute, was established about a year later. A branch reading room was housed here prior to the opening of Langley library in 1908.

OLDBURY AND LANGLEY GREEN STATION in 1968, showing the junction of the former Oldbury Railway in the foreground. This branch opened to goods traffic in 1884 and to passengers the following year. The passenger service was withdrawn as early as 1915, but it remained open for goods until 1964 and a short section continues to serve Albright & Wilson's chemical works.

SHOWELL'S BREWERY FIRE ENGINE *LILLIAN* after the fire at Langley Maltings on 25 and 26 September 1925. The brewery was established in 1870 on the site of an ancient medicinal spring known as the Wells of the Cross.

THE ROYAL OAK, Causeway Green Road, prior to rebuilding. Langley Green Road is to the right of the picture.

THE ORIGINS OF THE ZION INDEPENDENT CHAPEL, in Langley Green Road, can be traced back to around 1775, when a minister from the Moravians began to visit the district to preach under a tree. Services were later held at Langley Mill and in a barn near Smethwick Old Church. When they were evicted from the barn the congregation moved to a cottage on the site of the Merrivale public house and, later, to a thatched cottage in Langley Green Road, close to the site of the first chapel which was built in 1798. This was replaced in 1828 by the building shown on the right. In 1878 a much larger chapel was erected (below) which survived until 1975. The present United Reformed Church sanctuary stands on the site.

VIEW OF LANGLEY from Barnford Hill in 1935, showing the juxtaposition of modern housing and nineteenth century industry in the area. Langley Maltings and Crosswells Brewery can be seen towards the right of the picture.

SECTION THREE

Warley

LEAHOUSE FARM, in Pound Road, was one of four farms in the district purchased by George Whitehouse towards the end of the last century. Farming at Leahouse ceased in 1947 when Whitehouse's three daughters sold the property and moved to Wythall. The farmhouse, which was built around 1890, remained standing until the 1960s.

WARLEY WIGORN SCHOOL, at the junction of Beeches Road and Bristnall Hall Road, was one of the oldest schools in the Midlands. It was founded by John Moore and erected in 1730. The top view shows the building around 1860. It was used as a school until 1883 but remained standing until 1956, by which time it had been altered considerably (below). The Beeches public house now occupies the site.

COOPER'S FARM, at Hill Top, in 1931. The upper view shows the farmhouse, and the lower view the gateway leading to the outbuildings and piggeries on the opposite side of Hill Top Road. The Cooper family also farmed the nearby Bristnall Hall Farm.

GEORGE ROAD, from the Plough Inn around 1930 (above), and looking towards Pottery Road and the George Hotel in December 1927 (left). The corrugated iron building on the left of the upper photograph is St Katherine's Mission church which belonged to the parish of Christ Church, Quinton.

THE GEORGE HOTEL, at the junction of George Road and Pottery Road, was in existence by 1830. A new public house bearing the name was opened in 1937 on the opposite side of the road, but the old building remains standing and is now divided into shops. This view dates from 1927.

PREFABRICATED HOUSES between Wolverhampton Road and Romsley Road in 1947. Yardley Close now occupies the site.

HAYRICKS AT BRANDHALL FARM in 1945.

BRANDHALL GOLF COURSE, shown here in 1935, was laid out on fields which had formerly belonged to Brandhall Farm. The farmhouse, seen in the background, was probably an outbuilding belonging to Brand Hall, the seat of the Fokerham family, Lords of the Manor of Warley.

THE FIRST BLOCK of four houses erected in Brandhall Road (now Brennand Road) on the Perry Hill estate in 1949 by Smethwick Corporation under the Apprentice Master Scheme, showing the apprentices who took part.

KINGSWAY ESTATE, showing five-storey blocks of flats under construction at the junction of Queensway and Aldridge Road in 1962.

BLEAKHOUSE ROAD, looking towards the junction with Wolverhampton Road, in 1936. St Hubert's Roman Catholic church, built during the previous year, can be seen in the distance.

PERRY HILL LANE, looking towards Hagley Road West around 1930.

WOLVERHAMPTON ROAD, looking north-west towards Bleakhouse Road, in 1927, a few months before it was opened. The photograph below was taken in 1935, looking south-east from Bleakhouse Road. Considerable housing development had taken place by this time.

They put cables a post across this road during the war supposely to stop enemy aircraft landing

JAMES TURNER, BASKET MAKER (second from right) with a group of his workmen at Birch Road before the First World War. Mr Turner's son, Charles, was still making baskets in the area on a small scale as recently as the 1960s.

WARLEY ODEON CINEMA, at the junction of Hagley Road West and Wolverhampton Road, opened in 1934. Built in the Odeon style of the period, it was one of the largest cinemas in the district. The last film was shown in 1961, but the building became a bowling alley and survived for a further twelve years. An office block now stands on the site.

Went to the cinema many times

HAGLEY ROAD WEST (formerly Beech Lanes), looking west from Beechwood Road, in 1960. The road is now a dual carriageway. *out of Birmingham towards Halesowen.*

BAPTIST CHAPEL, in Hagley Road West, built to serve the small settlement at Beech Lanes in 1824. The congregation later merged with the White Ribbon Group to form Warley Baptist Church and a new chapel was opened in Castle Road East in 1935, a few years after this photograph was taken. The old building was used as a warehouse and auction room for around thirty-five years before being demolished.

WARLEY WOODS (above) is a landscaped park laid out in the 1790s by the prominent landscape gardener, Humphry Repton, for the then owner of the estate, Samuel Galton. Galton's son, Hubert, was responsible for building the Gothic Hall, popularly known as Warley Abbey, which was completed in 1819. It is seen (below) shortly after the estate was acquired by Birmingham Corporation in 1906 for use as a public park.

WARLEY ABBEY was used in later years as a golf club house. It was in a poor state when the photograph (above) was taken in 1955 and only survived a further two years. The lower view shows demolition work in progress at the rear of the building in May 1957.

THE GRECIAN TEMPLE which stood in the bluebell wood facing Warley Abbey. It was pulled down soon after the woods were opened to the public. The photograph dates from 1903.

TOBOGGANING IN WARLEY WOODS PARK in February 1956.

NORTH LODGE AND POOL at the Abbey Road entrance to Warley Woods Park. The lower photograph shows children playing in the pool in the summer of 1921.

HAYMAKING AT WARLEY HALL FARM (above) around the turn of the century when the Summerton Brothers were tenants. In later years the farm was run by Edward Morris. The lower view shows cows grazing in one of the fields alongside Pottery Road in 1929 with the farm buildings in the distance.

POTTERY ROAD in 1928, showing houses under construction. The upper view is from the junction with Abbey Road and the lower view from Harborne Road.

Pheasant Inn, Warley.

THE PHEASANT INN, in Abbey Road, was one of the most popular in the district, particularly in the years before the First World War when the licence was held by the genial Roland Ray. At that time the building was also a farmhouse with a Dutch barn and land extending for some distance at the rear. The inn was renowned for its ales which were brewed on the premises using water drawn from a well in the grounds. Other attractions included a shooting range, a skittle alley constructed by Mr Ray himself, a summer house, and rose gardens which supplied local gentlemen with their buttonholes on Sundays. These combined to make it a popular meeting place, particularly for residents of the nearby Bearwood district. This postcard view shows the old building which was replaced by larger premises in 1938.

THE POOL in the grounds of The Pheasant (right) in 1901, looking north towards Hill Top. Now drained, the site is partly occupied by the gardens of houses in Telford Close. The tea garden (below) was photographed in 1928. Pottery Road and the area around the George Hotel can be seen in the distance.

BROOK COURSE (left), close to the point where the present Hurst Road and Norman Road cross. The photograph, taken on Boxing Day in 1927, was entitled 'Snow and Willows' by the photographer. The same group of trees may be seen in the middle distance towards the right of the lower photograph, taken in August 1929. The white field beyond was known as 'The Daisy Field'.

ABBEY ROAD, showing the group of cottages at the top of Hurst Lane (above) in 1910. Warley Woods Park is behind the fence on the left. The lower photograph, taken at the same spot some twenty years later, shows a striking transformation.

HURST LANE, from Abbey Road, in 1929. The lane followed the line of the present Trinder Road.

THE VIEW FROM SLATCH HOUSE FARM towards Hill Top and the Glory Hills.

ABBEY ROAD, seen from Three Shires
Oak Road, in 1903.

KATHERINE ROAD, looking north from Abbey Road, in 1928. The road was developed by
William Henry Jones, the occupier of Slatch House Farm, and named after his wife. Several
other roads in the vicinity were also named after members of his family.

OLDBURY UDC OPENED A READING ROOM in a house in Barclay Road to serve residents of the Warley Woods area in 1911. A small branch library was added two years later. The photograph was taken on 1 April 1928, the day the district was transferred to Smethwick County Borough.

HOUSING DEVELOPMENT IN THE AREA from the late 1920s rendered the Barclay Road library inadequate and a new library was built in Thimblemill Road in 1936 to serve the growing population. The exterior view dates from around the time of the opening in February 1937, while the photograph of the interior was taken in 1944 for the *Times Literary Supplement*.

THE REMAINS OF THE THIMBLE MILL around 1890. Originally a corn mill, it was converted to thimble making in the eighteenth century. In the 1830s it was used by W.W. Blyth for the cutting of files by machinery, the first application of a patent taken out in 1833 by William Shilton, of Birmingham. It reverted to a corn mill in 1845 when William Summerton took over.

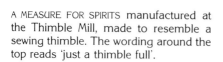

A MEASURE FOR SPIRITS manufactured at the Thimble Mill, made to resemble a sewing thimble. The wording around the top reads 'just a thimble full'.

THE MILL HOUSE (above), in Thimblemill Lane, and the rustic footbridge (below) across the brook at the point where it leaves the mill pool. Both photographs were taken shortly before the turn of the century. The pool survives as part of the recreation ground owned by G.K.N. plc, but the house and bridge have long since disappeared.

UNKETTS FARM stood beside a narrow lane leading from Thimblemill Lane to the Uplands, at Smethwick. It was photographed in 1925, a few years before the buildings were demolished.

THIMBLEMILL LANE (now William Road), looking towards Bristnall Hall Lane in 1925, following the realignment of the road. Bristnall Hall Farm can be seen in the distance.

HILL FIELD FARM, Thimblemill Lane, in 1936. The lower photograph shows part of the last litter of pigs to be reared at the farm.

WOODBINE COTTAGE stood in Queens Road at the junction with Thimblemill Lane. It was photographed shortly before demolition in 1930. The Two Brewers public house now stands on the site.

THE QUEEN'S HEAD INN, Londonderry, photographed early in the present century when it was owned by Cheshire's Brewery. The inn was replaced by a larger building during the 1920s.

Rowley Regis

ROWLEY VILLAGE in the early years of the present century, looking towards Blackheath, with the Swan Inn to the right of the picture. Since the 1950s the village has changed considerably and none of the buildings shown here remain.

THE ORIGINAL PARISH CHURCH OF ST GILES was built in the thirteenth century and stood until 1840 when it was pulled down and replaced by the building shown here. This second church had a brief existence as it was badly affected by mining subsidence and had to be closed in 1894. Most of the structure was subsequently demolished, although part of the tower was incorporated in the third church which was completed in 1904.

THE THIRD CHURCH LASTED ONLY NINE YEARS before its destruction by fire in 1913, the aftermath of which is shown above. Suffragettes were blamed at the time, but this was never proved and the true cause of the fire remains a mystery. The present structure, shown below in 1967, was completed in 1923.

THE VICARAGE AT ROWLEY, which stood in its own grounds adjoining the churchyard, was built with proceeds from the sale of the glebe land in 1841. It was replaced by the present building in Hanover Road in the mid-1960s.

CLUB BUILDINGS, off Hawes Lane, in 1971. In the nineteenth century these buildings were occupied by nailmakers and Jew's harp makers.

ROWLEY HALL COLLIERY began producing coal around 1870. The first proprietor was Frederick North, father of the stage designer, Paul Shelving, and the actor, Grosvenor North. During this period the North family lived at Rowley Hall. The colliery was acquired by Walter Bassano, Chairman of Rowley Regis Board of Health, in 1892 and later came into the ownership of H.S. Pitt & Co., who also owned the nearby Bell End and Ramrod Collieries. It was abandoned in 1919.

THE CABLE-OPERATED INCLINED RAILWAY (above) linking Rowley Hall Colliery with the canal basin at Whiteheath (below), where coal was loaded manually into boats.

Housing estate now along cide neatarway. Whiteheatl flat run where horses are in background. As a lad we used coal puch on the banks on left.

Used to easin in Thes eanal same - no boats here f came when I was a lad a stream used to run where the railway above is shorm.

PORTWAY HALL stood on the south side of Newbury Lane, close to the 'Four Ways' and the boundary with Oldbury. The building had sunk some twenty feet over the years as a result of the extraction of the thick coal beneath it. It was built in 1671 and had a timber frame, plastered over in the early nineteenth century, which probably saved it from collapse. These photographs, showing the exterior and the ornamental tiles in the porch, were taken in 1979, shortly before demolition.

EDWIN RICHARDS QUARRY (above), photographed in 1969 with Portway Farm, a late medieval farmhouse, in the foreground. Below is Hailstone Quarry, operated by Tarmac Roadstone Ltd, in 1973. These two quarries have now been amalgamated, resulting in the closure of Turner's Hill Road, part of the original route between Rowley Village and Dudley.

HAILSTONE FARM AND FREEBODY FARM, near Turner's Hill, showing Hailstone Quarry in the foreground. Below is a closer view of Hailstone Farm. Since these photographs were taken in 1969 quarrying has encroached still further on Turner's Hill and the farm buildings have disappeared.

DOULTON & CO LTD established their works for the manufacture of drainpipes at Springfield in 1848. At one time the firm manufactured architectural terracotta and blue bricks, but later concentrated on the production of glazed sanitaryware. These photographs show old kilns awaiting demolition in 1969. The factory closed in 1979 and the site is now occupied by an industrial estate.

Blackheath

MARKET PLACE, seen from Long Lane, in the 1950s. Blackheath Market is on the right.

The father of a friend of mine was killed on this corner

BIRMINGHAM ROAD in the 1950s, looking north from Market Place (above) and south from Regis Road (below). Blackheath bypass now runs between the Methodist church and the Market Place and many of the buildings shown here have been demolished.

HIGH STREET, from the Market Place, in the 1920s (above) and the 1950s (below).

I was a paper boy at the shop next door to the one on the left corner

THE PREMISES OF R. CUTLER, SHOE REPAIRER, at 110 High Street around 1930.

THE MANCHESTER HOUSE, on the corner of High Street and Heath Street, shortly before it was demolished to make way for a larger building in 1937.

MINCING LANE in the 1920s. Parts of the district still appeared quite rural at this time.

LICENSEE WILLIAM TAYLOR posing in front of the Pear Tree Inn, in Mincing Lane, around 1930.

GWR 2–8–0 NO. 3819 ENTERING THE TUNNEL between Blackheath and Old Hill with a tanker freight in August 1962. The Stourbridge Extension Railway from Old Hill to Galton Junction, Smethwick opened in 1867, completing a through route between Birmingham and Worcester.

We used play on this railway and tunnel and climbacres 16 A' frau

'CASTLE' CLASS 4–6–0 NO. 5014 *Goodrich Castle* at Rowley Regis and Blackheath station with the 5.40 p.m. Birmingham (Snow Hill)-Stourbridge Junction local train in June 1964. This was one of the few remaining steam-hauled services at that time.

SHUNTING LOCOMOTIVE at A.E.I. Ltd, Motor & Control Gear Division, now G.E.C. Electromotors Ltd, Cakemore Road, in 1967. The Shell petroleum distribution depot can be seen in the background.

THE M5 MOTORWAY, looking north from Cakemore Road in 1971, a year after opening.

SECTION SIX

Old Hill

AN EARLY VIEW OF THE CROWN INN, in Station Road, probably dating from the 1870s. The building has altered considerably since this photograph was taken.

HADEN HILL COLLIERY NO. 1 PIT was sunk in 1834. Its first owner was Alfred Barrs of High Harcourt, but in the mid-1860s Walter Bassano became the proprietor. The coal seam in this district reached the exceptional thickness of 25 ft and there were several mines on both sides of the Dudley Canal. No. 1 Pit was finally abandoned in 1913. This view dates from 1891.

LOADING COAL INTO BOATS at the canal wharf at Haden Hill Colliery.

Why didn't they tip the coal direct into the boats?

COKE OR 'GLEDE' OVENS on top of the huge pit mound known as 'Barr's Bonk' at Haden Hill Colliery. The site is now occupied by Waterfall Lane Trading Estate.

THE CABLE-OPERATED RAILWAY connecting No. 2 Pit with the main colliery at Haden Hill. Old Hill GWR station can be seen in the distance, with Waterfall Lane pumping station beyond.

CHIMNEY STEEPLEJACKS AT WORK at Haden Hill No. 2 Pit. This mine was sunk in 1865 alongside Halesowen Road, close to the home of its owner, Walter Bassano. Trees and shrubs were planted around the pithead to screen it from the house, causing it to be nicknamed 'The Pretty Pit'.

HADEN CROSS, home of the Bassano family, showing the courtyard and stables (above) and the music room (below). The building is now the headquarters of A. & J. Mucklow Ltd, building contractors.

HADEN HALL, the Tudor home of the Haden family, which is currently being restored. It is seen (above) at the turn of the century and (below) in 1967. The family were prominent in the district from the twelfth century until the death of George Alfred Haden-Best in 1921.

HADEN HILL HOUSE, adjoining the Tudor Hall, was built by G.A. Haden-Best in 1878 and the grounds were landscaped at the same time. The estate was purchased by public subscription and presented to Rowley Regis Council for use as a park in 1922. These views of the house and pool date from 1963 and 1890 respectively.

OLD HILL was once a railway junction of some significance, as the station nameboard in the view above indicates. The main line from Stourbridge to Galton Junction, Smethwick opened throughout in 1867 and the two branch lines which converged at Old Hill both followed in 1878. In the upper view 0–6–0 pannier tank No. 6422 stands at Old Hill with a train to Dudley in 1961, while the lower photograph shows sister locomotive No. 6424 approaching the junction with a train from Dudley in 1963.

0–4–2T NO. 1438 PROPELS A TRAIN from Dudley to Old Hill at the somewhat dilapidated High Street Halt in December 1956. The branch to Blowers Green Junction closed in 1964.

PASSENGER SERVICES ON THE HALESOWEN BRANCH ceased as early as 1927 due to competition from motor buses. The line closed completely in 1969 and little trace now remains. The photograph shows a train from Halesowen about to enter Haden Hill tunnel at the turn of the century.

HOLY TRINITY CHURCH, seen from Lawrence Lane, around 1893. The church was built in 1876, largely through the generosity of Walter Bassano, Chairman of Rowley Regis Board of Health. The Board of Health offices can be seen to the left of the photograph. On the right is Mark Round's cooperage, and in the distance, beyond Halesowen Road, the Black Waggon Colliery.

FIVE WAYS in April 1953. The buildings on the right of the picture have been demolished in recent years to enable road improvements to be made.

YE OLDE CROSS, in Halesowen Road, photographed in 1967. Renamed Samuel's a few years ago, this public house recently closed following a serious fire.

Cradley Heath

THE WORKSHOP OF EDWIN SHIRT, carpenter, joiner and coffin maker, in a disused chapel in Graingers Lane, around the time of the First World War.

UPPER HIGH STREET, looking towards Reddal Hill Road, showing the Bridge Inn (left) and Cradley Heath Library (right), prior to the First World War. The library opened in 1909, together with buildings at Blackheath and Tividale, and was the gift of Andrew Carnegie to Rowley Regis Urban District.

HIGH STREET, looking towards Five Ways, in 1971, showing Christ Church (Methodist) in the distance.

HIGH STREET, from Five Ways, around 1910 (above), showing the Talbot Hotel to the left of the picture. The lower photograph was taken from a similar viewpoint in 1968.

CRADLEY HEATH MARKET was opened in 1928. Prior to 1922 the market had been held in the High Street. The photographs were taken in November 1967 shortly before closure. A new market hall opened in 1969.

FIVE WAYS in 1953, looking towards High Street (above) and towards Cradley Road (below).

CHAINMAKING AT THE WORKSHOP OF HARRY STEVENS in Oak Street around 1912. Small chains were later manufactured using machinery, as in the photograph (below) taken at the Eagle Chain Works of Samuel Woodhouse & Sons Ltd, in Corngreaves Road, in the 1930s. This company, established in 1870, is one of several chainmakers still operating in the Cradley Heath district.

THE LONGEST MINE CHAIN EVER MADE. It was manufactured by Eliza Tinsley & Co. of Reddal Hill Road.

THE WORKSHOP OF H. BLUNT & CO., WELDERS, at the junction of Corngreaves Road and Prince Street (formerly King Street) in 1969. The site is now occupied by housing.

THE NEW BRITISH IRON COMPANY, whose Corngreaves Works are shown above, was established in 1825 and by the 1870s had become one of the largest industrial concerns in the Black Country. In addition to the iron and steel works, the company owned several coal and ironstone mines in the area and operated an extensive network of mineral railways connecting their various undertakings. The firm went bankrupt in 1893 as a result of the general depression in the iron trade in the region during the latter part of the last century. An attempt was made to sell the entire concern as one lot, but no satisfactory offers were received and the conglomerate was broken up and sold off in portions. The iron works, together with the Fly and Black Waggon Collieries, were taken over by the Corngreaves Furnace Company in 1894. For a short period the proprieter of the new company was Walter Bassano, the Chairman of Rowley Regis Urban District Council. The Corngreaves Works were demolished in 1927 and the site is now occupied by a trading estate. The photographs on these two pages date from the late 1890s.

BLAST FURNACES AT THE CORNGREAVES WORKS. The New British Iron Co. had two large Siemens Martin blast furnaces which formed part of the 'New Plant' described in the sale particulars of July 1893.

CORNGREAVES HALL dates mainly from the late eighteenth century, although it is possible that there was an earlier building on the site. It was originally the home of James Attwood, an uncle of the political reformer, Thomas Attwood, who founded the Birmingham Political Union for the Protection of Public Rights. James Attwood's son, John, sold the estate to the New British Iron Company in 1826 and the hall acted as the manager's house until the company went bankrupt in 1893. It became the property of Rowley Regis Borough Council in the early 1950s and is currently being restored by Sandwell Council. This view dates from 1969.

MABEL WAS BUILT FOR THE CORNGREAVES FURNACE COMPANY in 1899 by W.G. Bagnall Ltd of Stafford. This narrow gauge locomotive spent its entire existence working on the railway system of the former New British Iron Company, particularly the branch between Corngreaves Iron Works and Fly Colliery. It appears to have been scrapped in the mid-1920s.

A KIDDERMINSTER-BIRMINGHAM-LICHFIELD train arriving at Cradley Heath station in 1977. The station has since been rebuilt and the two platforms, formerly staggered on either side of the level crossing, now face each other.

MEREDITH STREET (above) and Hingley Street in 1971. The houses have since been demolished.

SECTION EIGHT

Tividale

CITY ROAD (formerly Gipsy Lane), near the Barley Mow Inn, around 1930. The antiquated petrol pump bears the legend 'Pratt's Gasoline'.

OAKHAM ROAD, from Darby's Hill Road, showing 'Hangman's Tree' and the cottage behind it which was once the home of George Smith, the notorious Dudley hangman. Beyond the row of cottages is Wellfield House. The photograph dates from around 1930.

DARBY'S HILL ROAD, from City Road, around 1930. The house in the distance, on the right hand side of the road, was used as a meeting place by members of Oakham Evangelical Church from 1872 until their own building was erected at the junction of Turners Hill and Portway Hill in 1905.

HAINGE FURNACES AND COLLIERIES, operated by Round Brothers, were situated beside the old Birmingham Canal. Their large slag heap at the side of the Dudley Road was a conspicuous landmark in the district. The furnaces went out of production around the turn of the century and were subsequently dismantled.

LONDON WORKS STEEL CO. LTD opened their Greenfels Works at Tipton Road in 1963. Production at the steel rolling mill expanded during the 1970s, but the works closed in 1982 and were subsequently sold.

PROTOTYPE 'TIVIDALE' SINGLE-DECK TRAMCAR (South Staffordshire Tramways No. 2) constructed at the Tividale works of the Birmingham & Midland Tramways Joint Committee in May 1917. The car was designed by Richard Humphries, Engineer to the Joint Committee, and

EY WEST BROMWICH & HANDSWORTH

BIRMINGHAM & MIDLAND
TRAMWAYS
JOINT COMMITTEE
CONSTRUCTED AT
TIVIDALE WORKS
MAY. 1917

was the forerunner of a type which was to operate successfully on various routes throughout the Black Country. The Tividale works opened in 1907, following electrification of the tramways, although no cars were actually built there prior to 1913.

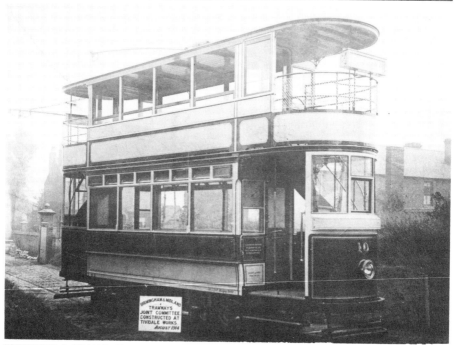

BIRMINGHAM & MIDLAND TRAMWAYS JOINT COMMITTEE STANDARD DOUBLE-DECK CAR NO. 10 on display at Tividale works where it was constructed in 1914.

THE LAST DAY OF TRAMCAR OPERATION, 30 September 1939. Birmingham car No. 136 is seen in Dudley Road West, passing the entrance to Tividale works. The works had not been used since Birmingham Corporation took over the operation of the service in 1928.

SECTION NINE

People

THE WEDDING OF ZACHARIAH COLE AND ANNIE STURMAN at Blackheath in September 1900. The exact location of the thatched cottage is not known.

GIRLS' CLASS AT WHITEHALL ROAD SCHOOLS, Cradley Heath, around 1922.

CLASS AT HAWES LANE CHURCH OF ENGLAND SCHOOL, Rowley Regis, around 1930.

NURSERY CLASSROOM AT MOAT FARM INFANTS' SCHOOL, Langley, which opened in October 1938.

MAYPOLE DANCING AT BLEAKHOUSE ROAD JUNIOR SCHOOL in 1957.

WILLIAM ERIC HOLLIES, the Old Hill cricketer, is perhaps best remembered for bowling out Don Bradman in his last test innings for no runs in 1948. Hollies played for Warwickshire from 1932 until his retirement in 1957, and for England in the mid-1930s and after the war. One of the finest bowlers of his generation, he continued to play for the Old Hill team until he was well over sixty. He died in 1981 at the age of sixty-eight.

CRADLEY HEATH FOOTBALL CLUB at the Dudley Wood ground, with Teddy Gray (second row, third from left), the well known Dudley confectioner, on 12 November 1949. After the photograph was taken, the team played Walsall 'A', winning by four goals to two.

REX WILLIAMS, of Blackheath, photographed in January 1948 on becoming the All England Boys Billiard Champion at the age of fourteen. He was later to become one of the leading billiard players of the post-war era, holding the World Professional Championship title between 1968 and 1980 and again in 1982 and 1983.

CHARLES THOMAS BARLOW, prominent industrialist and Mayor of Oldbury from 1942 to 1945. The founder of Accles & Pollock Ltd and London Works (Barlows) Ltd, C.T. Barlow was a notable local benefactor. He took a particular interest in Oldbury Repertory Players, whose theatre at Langley is named after him.

MRS. J.U. BARLOW, widow of C.T. Barlow, with Sir Barry Jackson at the opening of the Barlow Playhouse on 10 January 1956. The theatre was converted from the disused Spring Street Methodist chapel, at Langley, by members of Oldbury Repertory Players.

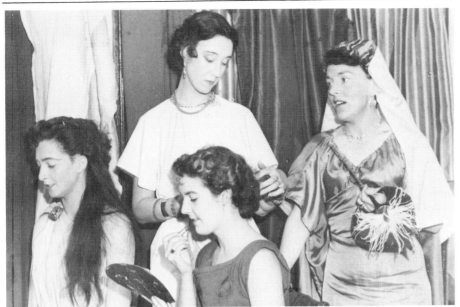

OLDBURY REPERTORY PLAYERS' production of *The Little Dry Thorn*, by Gordon Daviot, at the Little Theatre, Langley Institute in 1954. The photograph shows (left to right) Pam Smallwood, Sybil Ford, Pauline Duffield and Lucy Dawson in the dressing room before the final performance on 11 December.

A SCENE from the play *Lord Richard in the Pantry*, produced by Cradley Heath Secondary School in December 1955.

SIR JOHN FREDERICK BRIDGE, born at Parsonage Street, Oldbury in 1844, achieved fame as organist of Westminster Abbey, a position he held from 1875 until 1918. He was also noted as a composer of hymns and anthems and a writer on music, his best known book being his autobiography, *A Westminster Pilgrim*. A knighthood was conferred upon him in 1897 and he was Chief Musician at the Coronations of King Edward VII and King George V. He died in 1924 and was buried near his home in Aberdeenshire, Scotland.

THEODORE PEARSALL (1864–1880) was born at Popes Lane, Oldbury, and from an early age showed considerable promise as a violinist. He received instruction initially from his father and later from Mr Henry Hayward of Wolverhampton. In 1878 he entered the London Academy of Music as a student and such was his progress that two years later, on the recommendation of Charles Halle, he was sent to study under Professor Joachim at the Imperial Conservatory of Music in Berlin. It was there that his brilliant career came to an untimely end with his sudden death from 'palpitation of the heart.' He was buried at the Church of the Twelve Apostles, Berlin, but a monument was subsequently erected in Oldbury churchyard by his admirers as a tribute to his genius.

JACK JUDGE (1872–1938), fishmonger and entertainer of Low Town, Oldbury, with a song which he evidently hoped would emulate the success of his best known composition, *It's a Long Way to Tipperary*, written in 1912.

VICTORIA S.S. BAND, Old Hill, photographed in the early 1920s.

MEMBERS OF LANGLEY PRIZE BAND chairing their conductor, Dennis Masters, after winning the second section of the *Daily Herald* National Brass Band Championships at Kensington Town Hall in October 1957.

BOYS PLAYING WITH CLOCKWORK BOATS in a small pool close to the footpath which led from Queens Road to Hill Top, Warley. The site of the pool is now occupied by No. 36 Eva Road.

SONS OF REST posing in front of their pavilion at Birchley Park, Oldbury, in 1935. The Sons of Rest movement had its origins at Handsworth Park, Birmingham in the late 1920s, and subsequently spread throughout the district.

CHRIST CHURCH, Oldbury, New Peal of Bells Executive Committee, in 1887. The vicar, Revd W.T. Taylor, is second from left in the front row.

CLEMENT PASS (centre), pastor of the Zion Independent Chapel at Langley Green, sitting in front of the second (1928) chapel with Mr Jackson (left) and Mr Slim (right). A clockmaker by trade, with premises in Oldbury, Clement Pass was pastor at the chapel for forty-four years until his death in 1889 at the age of seventy-eight.

AN UNIDENTIFIED SOLDIER AND TWO GIRLS at the entrance to Warley Abbey around 1900.

MR BRETHERICK, the first park superintendent at Warley Woods, and his family in 1909.

ELIZA TINSLEY (1813–1882) was probably the most prominent female industrialist in the Black Country during the nineteenth century. She took control of her husband's nailmaking business at Cradley Heath on his death in 1851 and ran the company for twenty-one years with the result that it eventually became the largest manufacturer of wrought iron nails in Staffordshire. The firm, still known as Eliza Tinsley & Co. Ltd, subsequently concentrated on chainmaking and is now one of the largest representatives of a trade once common in Cradley Heath and the surrounding district.

LUCY WOODALL was the last woman in the Black Country to make chains by hand. She was born in 1899 and began her chainmaking career at Horton's, Old Hill on leaving school at the age of thirteen. She went on to work for William Stevens, of Netherton, and Harry Stevens, of Cradley Heath. From 1957 until her retirement in 1972 she was employed at the Eagle Chain Works of Samuel Woodhouse & Sons, where she was photographed at work in 1966. Mrs Woodall died in 1979.

WALTER WILLIAM HACKETT (1874–1964) was the first foreman at Accles & Pollock Ltd. He went on to become managing director, chairman, and eventually president of the Oldbury company. He was renowned for his wit and his fund of Black Country anecdotes. Many of these were published in verse form under his pen name 'Khanyer Whackett'.

ALAN 'CAGGY' STEVENS, one of the few remaining canal carriers, with his towing horse 'Mac', at his moorings close to the Whimsey Bridge at Halesowen Street, Oldbury in 1968. A well known character throughout the Black Country, he now operates from Owen Street, Tipton.

COLLIERY RESCUE TEAM which worked in mines owned by H.S. Pitt & Co. The company owned several collieries in the Rowley Regis and Dudley areas; this photograph is believed to have been taken at Knowle Colliery.

SECTION TEN

Events

THE OFFICIAL OPENING OF PERRYFIELDS COUNTY SECONDARY SCHOOL, Warley, on 14 September 1957. Alderman J.F. Goode is seen unveiling the commemorative plaque.

THIMBLEMILL BROOK, near Norman Road, Warley, during the flood of 14 June 1931.

DAMS WERE CONSTRUCTED across the Thimblemill Brook in 1932 to prevent the heavy flooding which occurred in 1927 and 1931 happening again. This photograph was taken immediately after a storm in July of that year. Norman Road can be seen in the distance.

CLEARING A PATH to the pig sties in Brandhall Lane, Warley, following a heavy snowfall in February 1947. Below is Moat Road on the same day, with Oldbury Grammar School in the background.

THE INCORPORATION OF THE BOROUGH OF ROWLEY REGIS, 28 September 1933. The photographs show the procession passing along High Street, Blackheath (above), and the Charter Town Clerk, Clifford Buckley, talking to the Rt Hon. George Lansbury MP, Leader of the Labour Party, at the Borough boundary in Tividale (below).

OLDBURY CHARTER DAY, 28 September 1935. The Macebearer is seen leading the civic procession (above) into Barnford Hill Park past the Territorial Army guard of honour. The Mayor and Mayoress, Cllr and Mrs K.H. Wilson, are shown inside the park (below), with Viscount Cobham walking behind.

GUN CARRIAGES UNDER CONSTRUCTION at Oldbury Railway Carriage & Wagon Works during the First World War.

UNVEILING OF THE WAR MEMORIAL at St Giles' church, Rowley Regis. The remains of the church, destroyed by fire in 1913, can be seen in the background.

THE 'GROW MORE FOOD' CAMPAIGN: demonstration plots at Barnford Hill Park, Langley in March 1940.

THE SPITFIRE presented by Rowley Regis Corporation during the Second World War.

AIR-RAID SHELTER at the junction of Hurst Road and Norman Road, Warley, photographed in 1946.

VE DAY CELEBRATIONS in Lawrence Lane, Old Hill, at the side of Palmer's fish shop.

CELEBRATIONS FOR THE CORONATION OF KING GEORGE V at Broadwell Park, Oldbury (above), and the procession at Station Road, Langley (below), on 22 June 1911. Showell's Crosswells Brewery is prominent in the lower view.

THE FORMAL OPENING of the new Wolverhampton Road by the Prince of Wales on 2 November 1927. The ceremony took place at the junction with Hagley Road West.

CORONATION DECORATIONS at the Excelsior Works of Thomas William Lench Ltd, bolt and nut manufacturers of Blackheath, in 1937.

Went past this works every day to school

RESIDENTS OF ALBRIGHT ROAD, WARLEY celebrating the coronation of King George VI on 12 May 1937.

A SACK RACE at Salop Road, Warley formed part of the coronation celebrations on 2 June 1953.

HER MAJESTY THE QUEEN AND HRH THE DUKE OF EDINBURGH visited Oldbury on 23 April 1957.
The procession is seen (above) turning into Wolverhampton Road from Bleakhouse Road
and (below) entering the Market Square.

CROWDS WAITING IN OLDBURY CHURCHYARD (above) for a glimpse of the Queen who is seen (below) being greeted by the Mayor, Cllr Alfred Gunn.

SILVER JUBILEE STREET PARTIES at Tower Road, Tividale (above) and Hadley Street, Oldbury on 7 June 1977.

THE OPENING OF THE LIBERAL CLUB in Birmingham Street, Oldbury, on 9 April 1910.

DECLARATION OF THE POLL for the North Worcestershire constituency in the general election of December 1910 outside the public buildings at Oldbury. Mr J.W. Wilson, the Liberal candidate, was re-elected on this occasion with a majority of 269 votes over his Unionist opponent, Mr Douglas Timins.

THE COAL STRIKE which affected the Black Country in 1912. Above: coal-picking near Ashes Road, Langley. Below: children at a soup kitchen at the Reindeer Inn, King Street (now Prince Street), Cradley Heath.

WORKERS from the Birmingham Railway Carriage & Wagon Works, Smethwick, demonstrating outside Oldbury Carriage Works on 28 May 1913. The demonstration was an attempt to persuade employees at the Oldbury works to join the strike which was affecting the Black Country iron trades at that time. Evidently it was successful as the works were closed the following day. The strike had originated at the Crown Tube Works at Wednesbury, and was to continue until July before a settlement was reached.

THE FOUNTAIN INN, in Albion Road, Oldbury, was the scene of a murder and attempted suicide on 1 April 1913 when the daughter of the landlord was shot by her lover after her father had refused his consent to their marriage. Having fired twice at the girl, the assailant turned the revolver on himself but, despite being badly injured, he survived to be tried and hanged at Worcester a few months later. His victim died of her wounds a week after the shooting at West Bromwich District Hospital. The photograph shows crowds gathering in the street outside the public house following the arrival of the ambulance.

WARLEY WOODS PARK on 9 June 1906 (above), the day it opened to the public, and (below) on the occasion of a Boy Scouts' demonstration in July 1909. Baden-Powell was in attendance at the latter event, his motor car being visible to the right of the photograph.

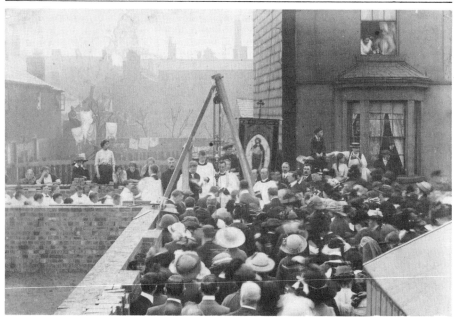

THE LAYING OF THE FOUNDATION STONE of the Parish Rooms at Church Square, Oldbury by the Archdeacon of Birmingham, the Revd Mansfield Owen, on 28 May 1913.

THE PRESIDENT OF THE METHODIST CONFERENCE, Revd W. Hodson Smith, laying the foundation stone of Warley Woods Methodist church on 7 July 1928. The church, which has recently been demolished, fell victim to structural damage as a consequence of its being built partly on the site of an old gravel pit.

THE OFFICIAL OPENING OF LANGLEY BATHS by Alderman H.H. Robbins, Chairman of the Estates Committee, on 8 May 1937.

WARLEY BRANCH LIBRARY, in Bleakhouse Road, was opened by Cllr H.A. Lacon, Chairman of Oldbury Libraries Committee, on 20 January 1938.

A CANAL TRIP for pupils of Park Senior Boys' School, Dudley and members of Tipton Road Methodist Guild, Tividale on 19 July 1952. The three narrow boats pulled by the motor boat *Susan* are seen leaving Tividale, on the old line of the Birmingham Canal, at the start of the five hour journey to Smethwick and back.

A CROSS COUNTRY RUN starting from Tividale Secondary School on 10 March 1956. The run of over two miles finished in Tividale Park. Eleven schools from South Staffordshire sent a total of sixty-four runners.

BLACKHEATH BENEVOLENT SOCIETY FETE on 21 September 1963. The procession (above) was the first to be held in Blackheath for over thirty years. It preceeded the annual garden fête at Westfield House, Hayseech, Old Hill (below).

FESTIVAL OF BRITAIN CELEBRATIONS at Oldbury in 1951, showing 'Queen Elizabeth' and courtiers in the Market Square.

ACKNOWLEDGEMENTS

The author is grateful to those photographers whose work appears in this book and to the many people who have donated photographs to the collection held by Sandwell Libraries. He is particularly indebted to the following who have provided information or given permission for photographs to be included:

Bob Binns • Mary Bodfish • Steve Cemm • John Dew • Michael Mensing
Sybil Mills • Robin Pearson • Tony Price • Ray Shill • Anne Young
Halesowen News & County Express • Mitchells & Butlers plc

The author would also like to acknowledge the support and encouragement of colleagues at Sandwell Libraries.